My
FIRST AID
Guide to...

CUTS AND BLEEDING

by Joanna Brundle

KidHaven
PUBLISHING

Published in 2022 by
KidHaven Publishing, an Imprint of Greenhaven Publishing, LLC
353 3rd Avenue
Suite 255
New York, NY 10010

© 2022 Booklife Publishing
This edition is published by arrangement with Booklife Publishing

Edited by: William Anthony
Designed by: Laura Gatie

Find us on

Cataloging-in-Publication Data

Names: Brundle, Joanna.
Title: Cuts and bleeding / Joanna Brundle.
Description: New York : KidHaven Publishing, 2022. | Series: My first aid guide to… | Includes glossary and index.
Identifiers: ISBN 9781534538108 (pbk.) | ISBN 9781534538122 (library bound) | ISBN 9781534538115 (6 pack) | ISBN 9781534538139 (ebook)
Subjects: LCSH: Wounds and injuries--Juvenile literature. | First aid in illness and injury--Juvenile literature.
Classification: LCC RC87.B78 2022 | DDC 617.17--dc23

Printed in the United States of America

CPSIA compliance information: Batch #CSKH22: For further information contact Greenhaven Publishing LLC, New York, New York at 1-844-317-7404.

Please visit our website, www.greenhavenpublishing.com. For a free color catalog of all our high-quality books, call toll free 1-844-317-7404 or fax 1-844-317-7405.

Photo Credits

All images are courtesy of Shutterstock.com, unless otherwise specified. With thanks to Getty Images, Thinkstock Photo, and iStockphoto.

Cover - bigjom jom, Rawpixel.com, Africa Studio, Amawasri Pakdara, Aha-Soft, Kwangmoozaa, piotr_pabijan, LightField Studios, New Africa, Nik Merkulov, Flas100. Whiteboard - piotr_pabijan. Grid - world of vector. Bandage Headings - Africa Studio. Page plaster numbers - Nik Merkulov. 1 - elenabsl, LightField Studios. 2 - elenabsl, iLoveCoffeeDesign. 3 - elenabsl, M.Stasy, iLoveCoffeeDesign. 4 - M.Stasy, Flas100, Sychov Serhii. 5 - Photographee.eu, M.Stasy, Aha-Soft. 6 - Bilanol, Flas100. 7 - M.Stasy, Phawat, Aha-Soft. 8 - nikiteev_konstantin, Andre Bonn, Vectomart, elenabsl. 9 - M.Stasy, Various photo, Aha-Soft. 10 - Patcharapa, Vectomart, elenabsl. 11 - takasu, elenabsl, Flas100, Vectomart. 12 - all_about_people. 13 - M.Stasy, Aha-Soft, David Pereiras. 14 - all_about_people, Vectomart. 15- Mega Pixel, Africa Studio, M.Stasy, Rtstudio, elenabsl. 16 - Melodia plus photos. 17 - nikiteev_konstantin, absolutimages, Aha-Soft. 18 - wellphoto, Vectomart. 19 - andreitlp, Aha-Soft. 20 - Andrey_Popov, Aha-Soft. 21 - Zdravinjo, Aha-Soft. 22 - temp-64GTX, Aha-Soft. 23 - spflaum, M.Stasy, Aha-Soft. 24 - elenabsl, iLoveCoffeeDesign.

CONTENTS

Words that look like <u>this</u> can be found in the glossary on page 24.

WHAT IS FIRST AID?

First aid is the help that is given to someone right after they have hurt themselves, had an accident, or become sick. Anyone can be a first aid hero, including you.

This boy is being helped by his friend.

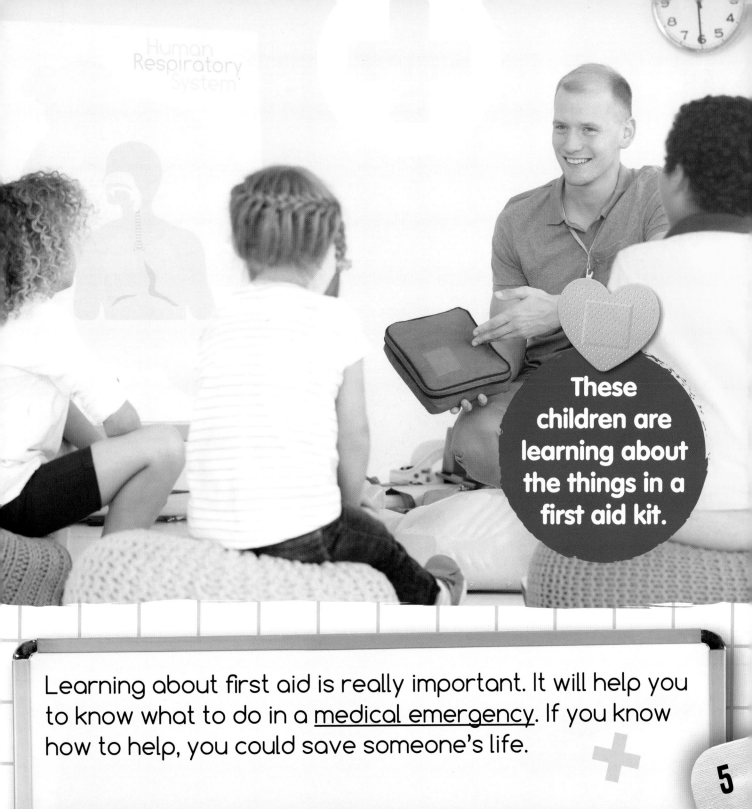

These children are learning about the things in a first aid kit.

Learning about first aid is really important. It will help you to know what to do in a <u>medical emergency</u>. If you know how to help, you could save someone's life.

WHAT IS BLEEDING?

Our hearts pump blood all around our bodies, including our skin. Skin has several layers. The second layer contains <u>blood vessels</u>. If we cut ourselves down to this layer, we bleed.

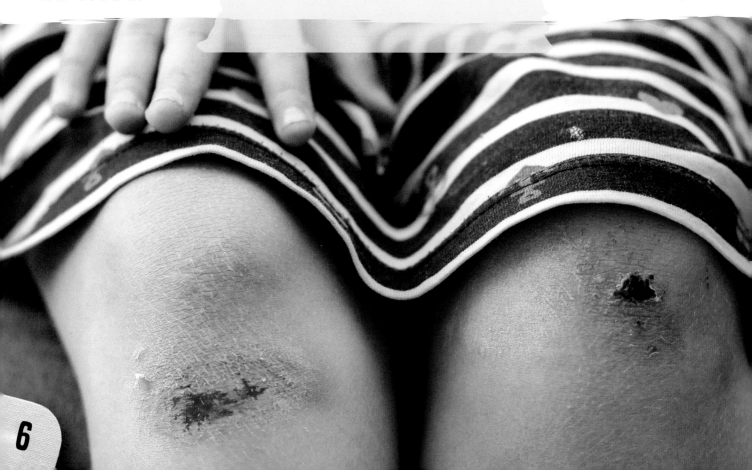

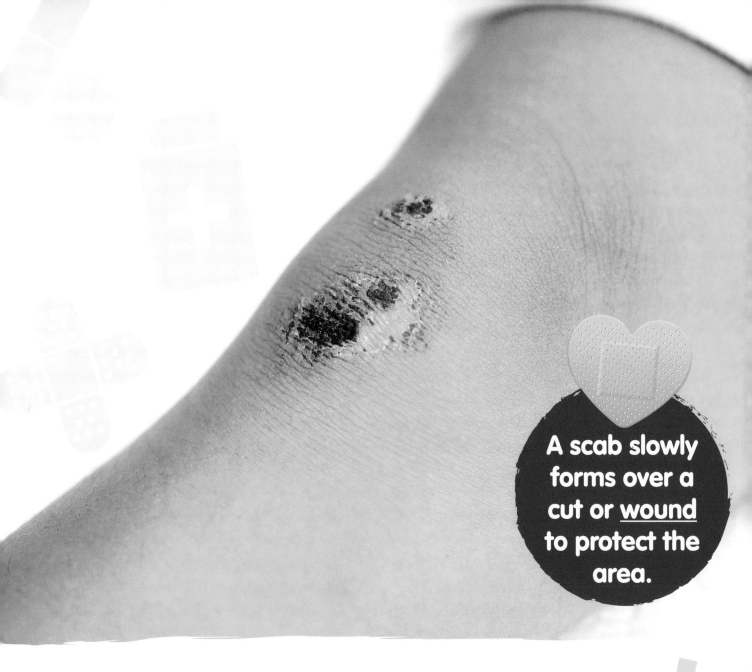

A scab slowly forms over a cut or <u>wound</u> to protect the area.

Blood contains tiny bits called platelets. These stick to the injured area and to each other. This makes a jellylike clump, called a clot. The clot closes up the break in the skin and stops blood from leaking out.

7

CUTS AND GRAZES

A cut is where the skin has been fully broken, usually by something sharp. This causes bleeding. A graze is where only the top layer of skin has been scraped away.

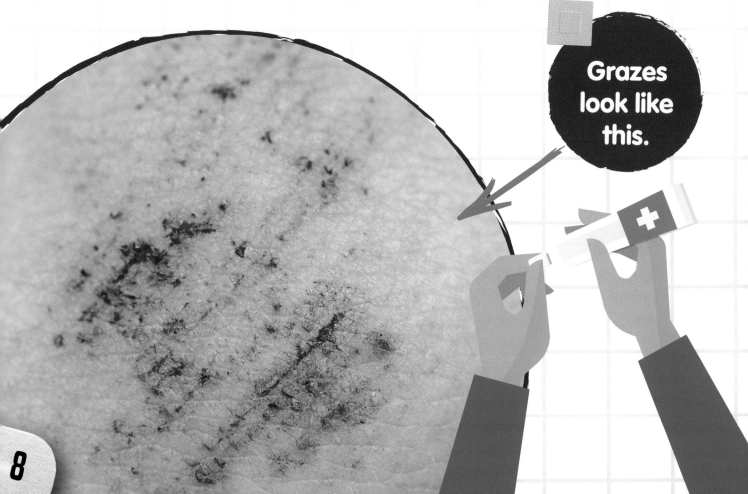

Grazes look like this.

Never try to remove glass from a wound yourself.

The injured person needs to see a doctor or nurse if:
- The bleeding doesn't stop
- You can see anything in the wound that shouldn't be there, such as glass

TREATING MINOR CUTS AND GRAZES

Minor cuts and grazes can usually be treated at home. To stop any bleeding, press gently on the wound using something clean and dry, such as a small towel.

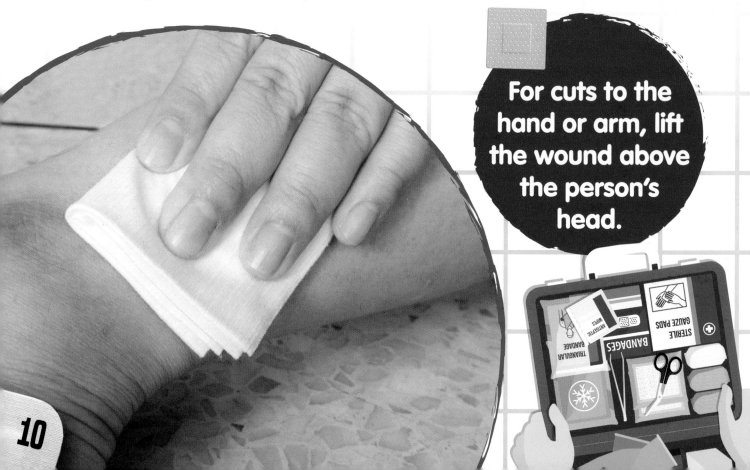

For cuts to the hand or arm, lift the wound above the person's head.

STERILE GAUZE PADS

BANDAGES

ANTISEPTIC WIPES

TRIANGULAR BANDAGE

Once the bleeding has stopped, clean the wound by holding it under running water. Dry the wound gently with a clean cloth or towel. Cover the wound with a clean <u>dressing</u>, such as a plastic <u>bandage</u>.

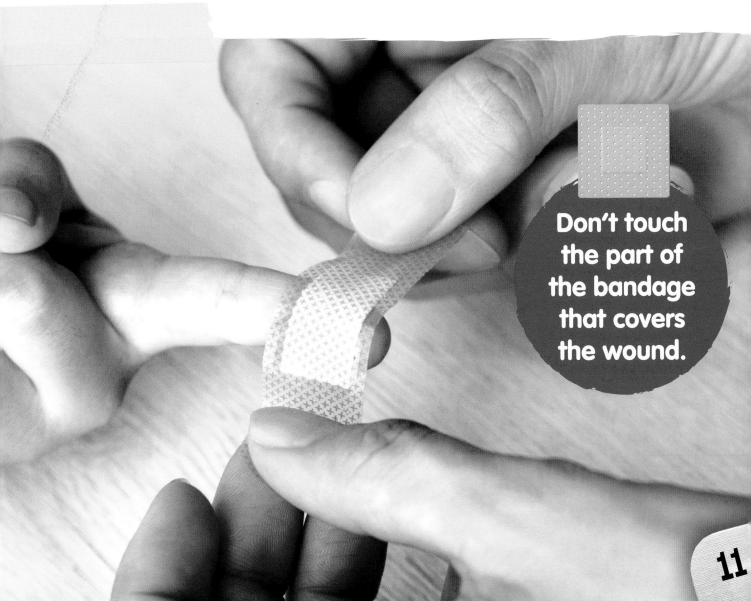

Don't touch the part of the bandage that covers the wound.

11

NOSEBLEEDS

If someone has blood coming from one or both nostrils, this means they are having a nosebleed. Nosebleeds are common but most are not serious. They can usually be treated at home.

Blood vessels in the nose are easily damaged, which can cause bleeding. Nosebleeds can be started by blowing or picking the nose. Being hit on the nose can also start a nosebleed.

Falling off your bike and hitting your nose could start a nosebleed.

TREATING NOSEBLEEDS

Ask the person to sit down rather than lie down. Ask them to lean forward, breathe through their mouth, and pinch the soft part of their nose.

Leaning forward makes the blood drain from their nose, so give them some tissues.

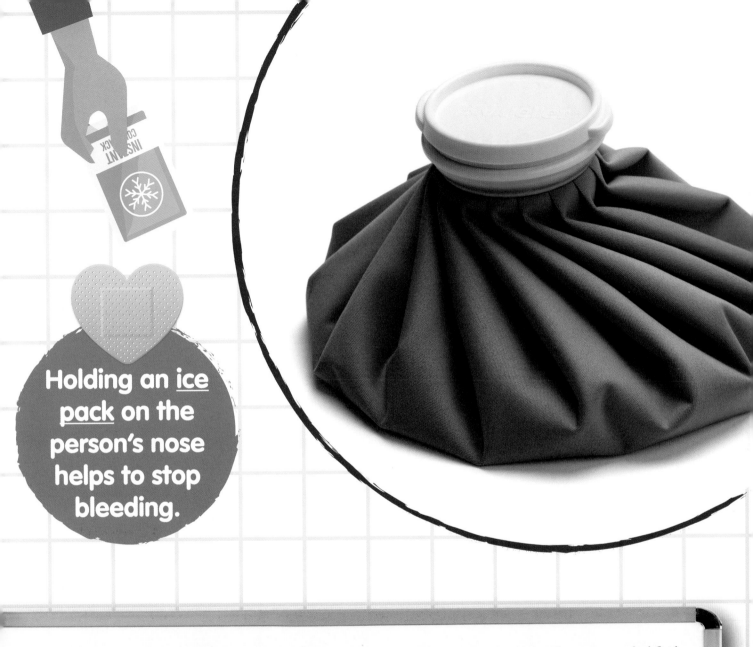

Holding an <u>ice pack</u> on the person's nose helps to stop bleeding.

After ten minutes, check if the bleeding has stopped. If it hasn't, they should pinch for another ten minutes. Call an ambulance if the bleeding is very heavy or hasn't stopped after 20 minutes.

15

TREATING SERIOUS BLEEDING

Take off any clothes that are covering the person's wound. Don't try to clean the wound. Put a dressing or clean cloth over the wound and press firmly with the <u>palm</u> of your hand.

If there is something in the wound, leave it there. Press around the wound rather than on it.

Bandage

First aid kits contain bandages and dressings.

Wrap another cloth or a bandage around the dressing or cloth. Try to wrap firmly, but not too tightly. Keep pressing with your hands if you don't have another cloth or bandage. Call an ambulance.

17

Help the person to lie down on a rug or blanket. Talk to them to keep them calm. Next, try to lift the injured part higher than their heart. This helps to stop the bleeding.

If you don't have a rug or blanket, use your coat or sweater.

18

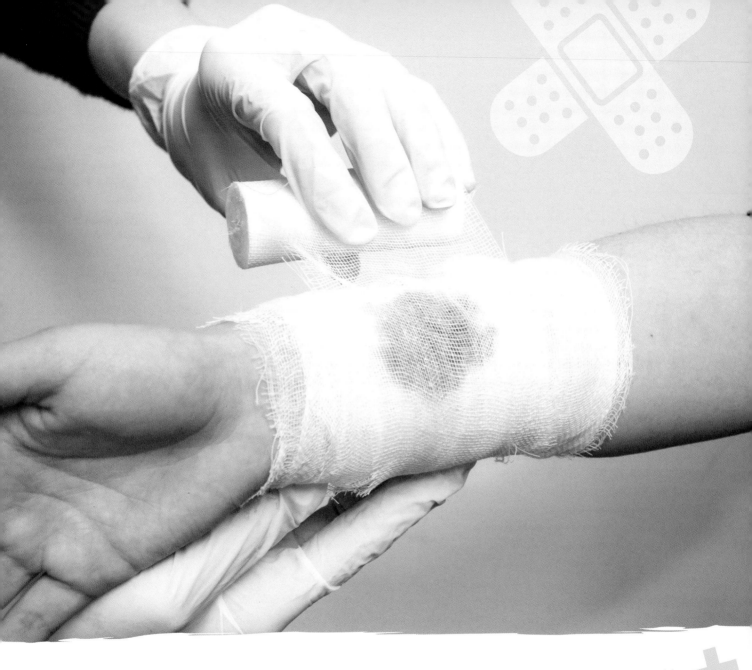

If any blood comes through the bandage, don't remove the
bandage. Add another one on top of the first one. Keep
pressing firmly on the area. Watch out for signs of shock.

SHOCK

Losing a lot of blood can make someone go into shock. Signs of shock include pale and cold skin, dizziness, fast breathing, and a fast <u>heart rate</u>.

Shock can be serious. Learning to treat shock could save someone's life.

First, call an ambulance. Lay the person down with their legs higher than their head, but don't move an injured leg. Loosen any tight clothing and use a coat or blanket to keep the person warm.

THINGS TO REMEMBER

You can call an ambulance by dialing 911 from any home phone or cell phone. Tell the <u>operator</u> where you are, giving the full address if you know it.

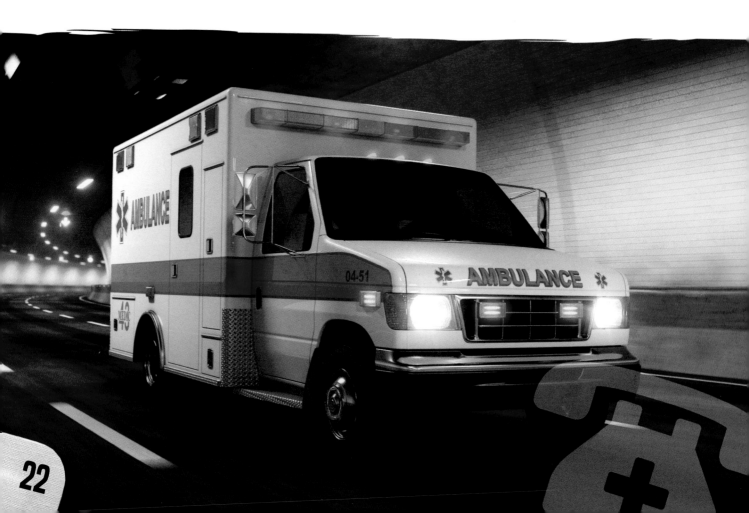

Blood can carry <u>diseases</u>. Wash your hands before and after helping someone who is bleeding.

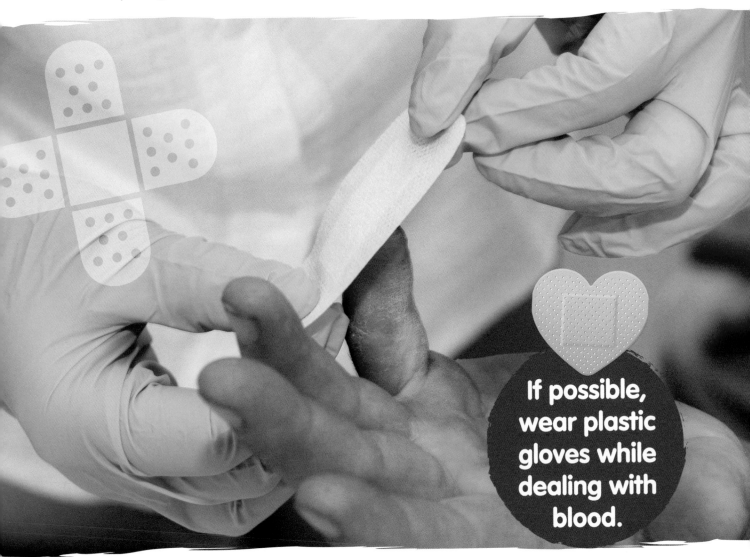

If possible, wear plastic gloves while dealing with blood.

If someone has thin, watery blood coming out of their nose after a bump on the head, call an ambulance right away.

GLOSSARY

bandage   a strip of material used to cover or wrap a wound

blood vessel   a part of a network through which the heart pumps blood around the body

disease   an illness that causes harm to the health of a person, animal, or plant, sometimes caused by germs

dressing   a piece of material used to cover and protect a wound

heart rate   the number of times someone's heart beats in one minute

ice pack   a bag filled with frozen things, or an item found in a first aid kit that gets very cold when it is squeezed or hit

medical emergency   a situation in which someone needs help from a medical professional right away

operator   the person who answers an emergency telephone call

palm   the inner surface of the hand, between the wrist and the fingertips

wound   an injury to the body in which the skin is broken

FIRST AID
EMERGENCY MANUAL

INDEX